I0467279

FREE GOOGLE:

Free SEO, Social Media, and AdWords Resources from Google for Small Business Marketing

A 299 GUIDE
2014 - 2015 EDITION

by Jason McDonald, Ph.D.
© 2014, JM Internet Group
www.jm-seo.org
510-713-2150

Table of Contents

Prologue

Before we begin...

This is a completely **unofficial** guide to Google resources. Google has not endorsed this guide, nor has Google nor anyone affiliated with Google been involved in the production of this guide.

That's a *good thing*. This guide is **independent**. My aim is to "tell it as I see it," giving you no-nonsense information on free marketing opportunities provided by Google.

In addition, please note the following:

- All trademarks are the property of their respective owners. I have no relationship with nor endorsement from the mark holders. Any use of their marks is so I can provide information to you.

- Any reference to or citation of third party products or services whether for Google AdWords, Google Webmaster Tools, Google Analytics, or any other Google product or otherwise, should not be construed as an endorsement of those products or services tools, nor as a warranty as to their effectiveness or compliance with the terms of service of Google.

The information used in this guide was derived in 2013, and updated in Spring, 2014. However, all Google products and services change rapidly, so please be aware that scenarios, facts, and conclusions are subject to change without notice.

Additional Disclaimer. Internet marketing is as much art as science. Any changes to your Internet marketing strategy, including SEO, Social Media Marketing, and AdWords, is at your own risk. Neither Jason McDonald nor the JM Internet Group nor Excerpti Communications, Inc., assumes any responsibility for the effect of any changes you may, or may not, make to your website or AdWords advertising based on the information in this guide.

Now that we've covered the background, *let's get started.*

0

Introduction

Welcome to *Free Google*, your unofficial, unauthorized but incredibly helpful guide to Google's free resources for SEO, Social Media, and AdWords. As part of the JM Internet Group's *299 Free Guides* series, *Free Google* orients you to **free** resources that Google produces for small business marketers. For example –

> Did you know that Google will give you a free website? That Google will alert you – for free – to mentions of your company across the Web or blogs? Or that Google has a tool called "Google Page Speed" that will test the speed of any web page, and give recommendations for improvement? Are you aware that *Google Takeout* will download and backup your Gmail, Google Docs, and other Google-based data?

Here's a big one – Even though **SEO** or **Search Engine Optimization** is all about getting to the top of Google for free, many small business owners or marketers do not know that Google produces an **official free SEO guide.** That's right – A *free* official guide by Google about getting to the top of Google, for *free*!

It's all there – for **free** – amidst the Googleplex. But there's a problem - a catch.

THERE MUST BE A CATCH!

So what's the catch? The catch is that despite the fact that Google is the world's number one search engine, Google does a **terrible, horrible, no good, very bad job** of explaining where all the free goodies are in the Googleplex!

That's where I come in. My name is Jason McDonald. I teach online marketing at corporate workshops, for my own company (the JM Internet Group), at Stanford University Continuing Studies and elsewhere in the San Francisco Bay Area. My mission is to make SEO, Social Media Marketing, and AdWords easy, fun and (to the extent possible), **free**.

In this *299 Free Guide*, I am going to give you a tour of the amazing, free but sometimes hidden, resources provided by Google for small business. Read this guide, and then circle back to pick and choose just those resources that will really help turbo-charge your company's Internet marketing strategy.

Let's get Started!

>> Bonus Appendix

>> Acknowledgements

>> Get Free Stuff

>> Links for Help and More Information

>> Copyright and Disclaimer

>> Bonus Appendix

But wait, there's more! Write an honest **review** of this Free 299 Guide on Amazon or elsewhere on the Internet, and I will send you the free **Bonus Appendix** of **all** the free Google resources for small business in easy, clickable format as a gesture of gratitude. Simply:

1. Write your review on Amazon or on your blog.

2. Contact me at http://jm-seo.org/299.

3. I'll email you the Bonus Appendix.

Thank you in advance for helping others locate fabulous, fun, and free resources for small business from Google!

>> Acknowledgements

I want to thank Noelle Decambra, my beloved wife, for her assistance in editing the guide and researching the materials as well as Gloria McNabb for her help covering phones and emails for an author too busy to do it all himself. I would also like to thank my students, who by their questions, enthusiasm, and puzzled looks have inspired me to never stop learning. Leonard Rogers of Acorn Studios (Sacramento, California) is responsible for formatting of this book. As usual, Len made a complex graphic design task seem easy.

>> Get Free Stuff

We produce a lot of free content at the JM Internet Group. Here's how to be alerted of free items as we produce them –

- Sign up for our **free** email alerts at http://jm-seo.org/free. Then, when we release a new *Free 299 Guide*, you will receive an email alert of our advance review copies.

- Take one of our **paid** training classes on SEO, Social Media Marketing, and/or AdWords. Everyone who takes our classes will have **free** access to **all** the guides in the series. (Find out more at http://jm-seo. org).

- Use a **coupon code**, available from someone who:
  (a) is already on our mailing list
  (b) purchased a copy of this guide, or
  (c) took our classes.

>> Links for Help and More Information

Here are important links for help and more information –

- **YouTube Videos** – "how to" videos on YouTube at http://www. youtube.com/jmgrp that give step-by-step instructions on important tactics for SEO, Social Media Marketing, and AdWords.

- **Free Webinars** – free introductory webinars on free SEO tools, Social Media Marketing tools, and AdWords tools; as well as monthly timely topics in Internet marketing at http://www.jm-seo.org/free.

4

- The **JM Internet Group** website at http://www.jm-seo.org/. Don't miss the free stuff, blog, and tips sections.

Questions? Email info@jm-seo.org, click http://jm-seo.org/44, or call 510-713-2150. As someone who loves to teach, I work really hard for my students and readers, so I strongly encourage you to email me with any questions. Don't hesitate!

~ Jason McDonald, Ph.D.

>> Copyright and Disclaimer

The Googleplex

The Googleplex is a physical place: Google's world headquarters is officially located at: 1600 Amphitheatre Parkway, Mountain View, CA 94043. In addition, the Googleplex is also the business of Google - a sprawling information e-business that serves consumers for free and makes over 96% of its revenue from paid advertising. The Googleplex is also a state of mind - an engineering mindset that builds amazingly powerful software, but often neglects to make that software user-friendly, or to write user manuals so that business owners can navigate from one Google product to another.

GOOGLE:
POWERFUL, FREE, AND COMPLICATED.

In this chapter, we will *first* overview Google's products for consumers and businesses and *then* zero in on marketing opportunities within the Googleplex, all at a bird's-eye view. In later chapters, we dive into the details of marketing opportunities across the Googleplex.

>> Google and the Consumer: Search

To most consumers, the mention of Google signifies a journey of discovery that begins at the colorful, if empty, search box at http://google.com/. Most consumers have little idea of the algorithm behind Google search, just as many business owners have only the vaguest of ideas about how this algorithm can be influenced to show one website over another (such is the quest called *SEO* or *Search Engine Optimization*). Yet behind the search algorithm lies a powerhouse not just of information but of marketing opportunities. (You can access an official Google informational resource on "how search works" at http://bit.ly/1hYRjjz).

Let's point out the basics of a typical Google page. Here's a screenshot of a Google search for "industrial fans":

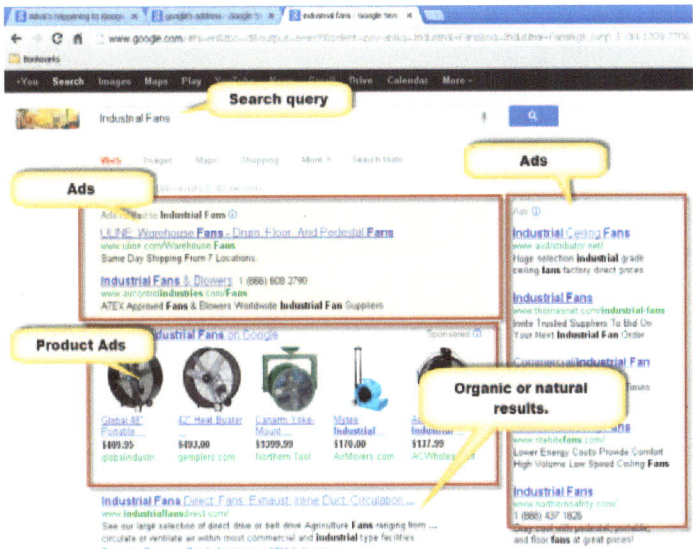

The basic layout is ads on the top and top right of the page, with the "natural" or "organic" results appearing beneath the ads. For certain types of queries, such as "industrial fans" Google also shows "product ads" - also called "shopping" ads via a subset of its AdWords advertising system called "Google shopping."

For other ads that have a local character such as "roofing company" Google shows Google+ Local listings, which is Google's online equivalent of the printed Yellow Pages. Here's a screenshot of a search for "roofing company" showing the Google+ Local listings:\

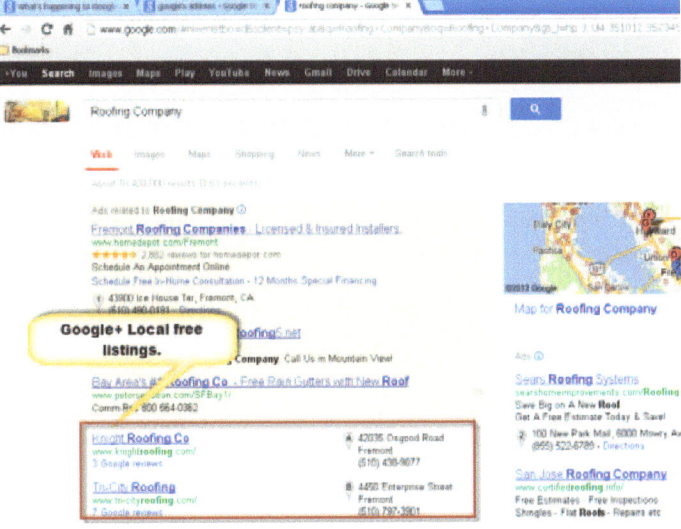

So from the consumer's perspective, Google is a search engine that displays its results in the following basic categories:

- **Ads** – appearing in the top middle and top right positions, sometimes showing product or "shopping" ads with pictures.

- **Organic or natural results** – non-paid ("free") results appearing beneath the paid ads.

- **Google+ Local results** – non-paid ("free") company listings appearing beneath the organic results, only on searches that have a local character.

From the small business perspective, in contrast, each of these categories presents marketing opportunities: **paid** ways to get to the top (advertising) as well as **free** ways to get there (SEO). Moreover, hidden in the Googleplex is a wealth of free tools and information resources that can help move you from *novice* to *expert* in how to leverage Google to get your marketing message to more customers for less money and effort!

>> Google and the Consumer: Social Media

Beyond basic Google search, Google is attempting to make a big splash in social media. We've already seen one of its social media endeavors – **Google+ Local**, which is Google's equivalent of the Internet Yellow Pages and a direct competitor to Yelp. Consumers can post reviews of any business, and they can read reviews posted by others. In fact, businesses that have more reviews as well as a good SEO-profile vis-a-vis Google+ Local show up higher and more frequently for relevant searches on Google, all for free! *(See Chapter 4 for more details).*

Google+ Local, in fact, is a primary component of Google Google's social media platform **Google+**: which has three amazing opportunities for small business. First, **Google+ profiles** for individuals, with picture rewards on Google search and better search positions. Second, **Google+ Local**, which we have touched on above. And third, **Google+ pages** for businesses, which is a direct competitor to Facebook. On Google+, as on Facebook, individuals can set up "profiles" whereby they can post and share with their Google+ friends (known as "circles"), and businesses can set up "pages" to talk with consumers. Google+ can be found at http:// plus.google.com/ *(For more about Google+, see Chapter 5).*

A final and very successful part of Google's social media strategy is YouTube (http://www.youtube.com), the video sharing site. YouTube is the largest video site in the world and the de facto second largest search engine on the planet, serving more searches than Bing *(For more about YouTube, see Chapter 6).*

>> Blended or Universal Search

Google now displays results in what is called "blended" or "universal" search results. What this means is that Google mixes and matches news, Google+ Local listings, ads, product ads, blog posts, YouTube videos, product review stars, and even pictures of Google+ authors on a simple search screen. It's important for business marketers to get into the habit of doing target searches and identifying all the available marketing opportunities.

The most common elements of blended search are:

- **AdWords** – paid ads on Google.

- **Google Shopping / Product Search** – paid product listings on Google.

- **SEO** – getting to the top of Google's free or organic listings.

- **Google+ Local** – getting to the top of Google's free "Yellow Page" listings.

- **YouTube Videos** – getting videos to show on Google search pages.

- **Google+ Authorship** – getting one's picture to show on a Google search result.

- **Microdata & Review Stars** – using microdata to transmit reviews and other data to Google, thereby getting stars and pictures on one's organic results on Google.

- **News** – getting press releases to show on Google's news service.

>> Other Google Products

Beyond search and social media, Google provides other products for both individual and business consumers such as **Google Apps** (free cloud storage and document apps) and **Google Play** (the equivalent of the Apple iStore). Since we are interested in small business marketing, we will focus only on those Google services that provide some sort of marketing opportunity. For a complete list of Google products go to http://jm-seo.org/299-g9.

>> Google and the Webmaster

Google depends on quality information from sites across the Web, and Google reaches out to webmasters to work with them on that information. It's not a perfect relationship, however, webmasters (as marketing professionals) would prefer to get to the top of Google properties for free using tactics like SEO, whereas Google would like everyone to *pay* via AdWords. So there is somewhat of a love/hate relationship between Google and webmasters behind the scenes of what otherwise appears to be a friendly public relationship.

That said, here are some of the basic services Google provides for webmasters:

> **Webmaster Tools** – a free service for webmasters sharing information about how their website is perceived by the Google search engine. Learn more at http://jm-seo.org/299-g11.

> **Google Analytics** – a free web metrics and analytics platform for webmasters that provides data on how users get to a website and what they do once they arrive. Learn more at http://www.google.com/analytics.

In addition, Google provides a few very important free tools for webmasters and Internet marketers to learn how users search the web, especially with regard to search keywords. The most important is the free Google keyword planner (http://jm-seo.org/299-g12); you can watch a free video on how to use it at http://bit.ly/kp-use. Google Trends is also useful at http://www.google.com/trends.

Google also has a program called AdSense (http://www.google.com/adsense) that allows high volume website publishers to serve Google ads on their websites and make money from clicks.

>> Google and the Advertiser

Google makes more than 96% of its money from advertising, via advertising, primarily AdWords (http://adwords.google.com/). However, there is more than one opportunity available with AdWords, namely:

Traditional AdWords, Search Network – ads being placed by pay-per-click bidding, and appearing on the Google search engine as well as search partners such as AOL (http://adwords.google.com/).

Traditional AdWords, Display Network – ads being placed by pay-per-click bidding, but appearing not on Google search directly but rather on partner blogs, portals, Gmail, YouTube and other browse able sites across the Internet, as well as via remarketing (http://adwords.google.com/).

YouTube – ads being placed on YouTube and elsewhere on the Internet (http://adwords.google.com/video).

AdWords Express – ads being placed on the Google Search Network and on the Display network but through a simpler, easier-to-use interface for small business local advertisers (http://www.google.com/places and http://www.google.com/adwords/express/).

Mobile and App Advertising – ads being placed on mobile phones as well as on the app marketplaces, including Google Play (https://play.google.com/store) and the Apple iStore.

Google Shopping or Merchant Center – ads being placed via product XML feeds and appearing on Google search as product ads (http://www.google.com/ads/shopping/).

As is always true with Google, don't expect one advertising property to alert you to another, and don't expect the user interface between them to be seamless! It's best to identify where you want your ads to appear on Google and work backwards!

>> Google and Help

In most cases, when you are "inside" a Google property such as AdWords or Webmaster Tools, "help" is available by clicking as follows on the top right of the page. First, click on the "gear" icon, and then on "help" in the pull-down menu that appears. Here's a screenshot:

As we shall see in this book, many of these properties (such as AdWords) have a wealth of free support and learning available, but Google does a **terrible, horrible, rotten, no good** job of connecting the advertising property and the learning sites. You have to know to look for them!

Beyond that, Google has a powerful **technical support supersite** at http://support.google.com/ and once you know it exists, you can type your questions right into a search box there and get answers across Google properties. A nifty tactic to search all of Google support is to first go to Google, and then enter *site:support.com {keyword}*. To find articles on "bounce rate," for example, you'd enter:

Note that there is **no space** between *site: and support.google.com*. This search will return **only** records located on the official Google support site.

There is also a plethora of Google **user forums** around topics like AdWords, Webmaster Tools, Analytics, etc., and you can find them here at http://jm-seo.org/299-g13. Simply browse what other users are asking, or post your own question for other users to answer. It's a free-for-all, so sometimes the answers are good, sometimes not so good, and all official Googlers are on their best behavior, sometimes (sadly) sacrificing truth or honesty in the name of good corporate public relations.

Another quick way to find a **user forum** is simply to go to Google and type in "user forum" plus whatever Google product you are interested in. For example, try typing this query into Google –

> *Google Analytics User Forum*

So often with Google, knowing the **question** is the first and most critical step to finding the **answer!**

>> Official Google Blogs and YouTube Channels

Almost every Google property such as YouTube, Webmaster Tools, Analytics, AdWords, etc. has official blogs and YouTube channels if you know to look for them. First, you have to know to look, and second you can't expect one Google product group to let you know where the other product group's stuff is. It doesn't work that way at Google.

There are, however, a few good master lists of blogs, YouTube channels, Google+ pages, and Facebook pages. You can get to them all here - http://www.google.com/press/ - simply click on the left hand side for a directory of blogs, YouTube channels, and the like:

2

Advanced Google

It seems so obvious when you think about it. Google is the world's number one search engine. **So why can't you use Google to find cool stuff by Google about itself?** In other words, is it possible to use Google search techniques to penetrate into the Googleplex and identify free marketing tools and opportunities. The answer is a resounding **"yes!"**

You can (and should), "Google Google."

Even better, with some tips and techniques you can become a power searcher, using Google to self-identify Google resources. Then, as a marketer you can "Google Google" to identify free Google marketing opportunities as well as tips, tricks, and techniques to be a Google marketing power user.

How cool is that?

>> Simple Google Search

The simplest way to find an answer to a Google-related question is to simply type the question into Google. Just go to Google and type your query. Let's assume your question is "What does Bounce Rate mean?" Here's how you might get some answers to that question via Google:

1. Go to Google (http://www.google.com/)

2. Type your question ("What is bounce rate") and hit enter.

3. Browse for relevant answers.

Here's a screenshot:

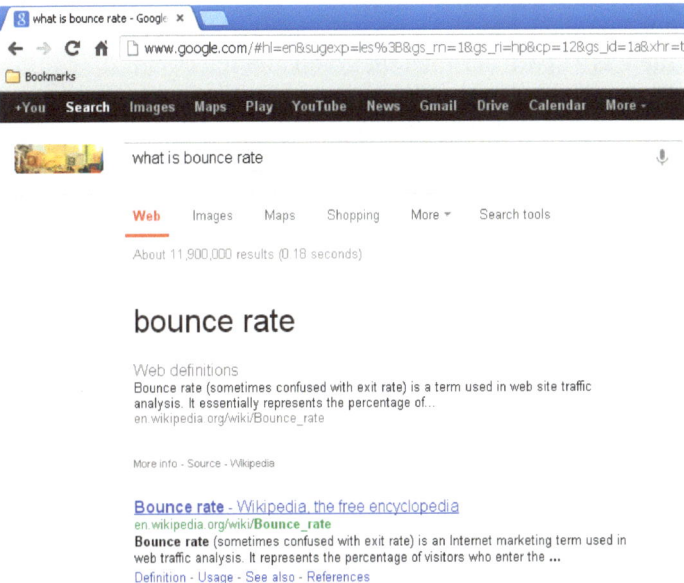

Pretty simple -right? But surprisingly many people don't think to just type directly into the Google search engine to get answers to their questions on how to market, for free, via Google.

>> Simple Advanced Search

Beyond just typing your question directly into Google, you can use some more advanced techniques to filter your results just to specific sites, especially "official" Google sites. Here's how:

Let's assume, for example, that you want to know the definition of a "landing page" in Google Analytics. And, let's say that you want to find only **official** Google answers to this question. You can use Google to filter just **official** Google pages. Using **Advanced Search** on Google is the way to do this. Here's how:

1. Go to Google (http://www.google.com/).

2. Type into the search box as follows:
site:google.com

3. Add your keyword / question
site:google.com what is a landing page in google analytics

Google will then return only results on Google.com (a.k.a., "official" Google pages) that address this query. Be sure to put **no space** between site: and the domain – as in site:google.com (**no space!**). It does not work if there is a space between the colon and the domain!

Here's a screenshot of it done correctly:

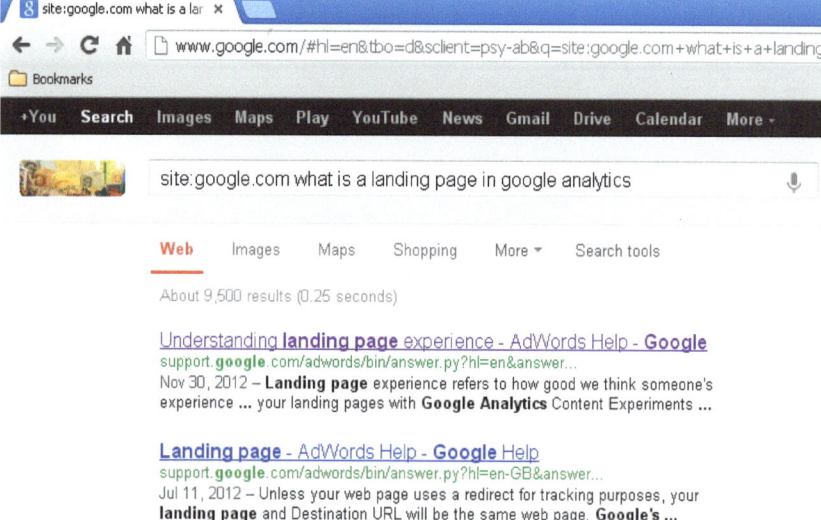

So, for example, you can type into Google site:google.com how to claim a Google local listing, or site:google.com how to set up a YouTube channel, or site:google.com how to get a picture to show on Google search, etc.

Another way to do this is to use **Google Advanced Search** directly. You can find *advanced search* hidden beneath the gear icon on the top right side of any Google search screen. Alternatively, just go to http:// www.google.com/advanced_search. Where it says *site or domain* simple type in *google.com* and you are restricting the results to official Google pages.

And, if you like shortcuts, you can find a complete list of Google search operators (symbols and commands) to add to Google searches at http://bit.ly/google-sops.

>> Help Within Google Properties

Another rather obvious thing to do is to search the **help functions** inside of Google properties. In **Google Analytics**, for example, help is located at the top right of the Google screen. Simply click it and type in a question.

This is true in **AdWords** and **Webmaster Tools** as well. "Help" is generally at the **top right** of the screen in all Google products!

Ask for Help!

So when you need help, ask for help!

Finally, the master **Google Support** site for help is https://support. google.com/. You can simply start at that site and search for help across all Google properties. Simply go to the **Google Support** site, find the icon of the Google property for which you need help, and browse for articles. Alternatively, enter *site:support.google.com {keyword}* into Google, and you can use Google to "Google" the Google support site.

Simple, right?

>> Google Alerts

You can use Google to alert you to new websites, blog posts, and other Web content that matches topics that interest you via its free Google Alerts system. For instance, let's say you are a hardcore AdWords advertiser and would like to stay informed of free Webinars on AdWords. You can use Google Alerts to email you alerts as it finds new webinars on AdWords. Here's how:

1. Sign in to your Gmail account.

2. Go to http://www.google.com/alerts **(Google Alerts)**

3. Type your search query into the box. For example, "Free Ad-Words Webinars" and hit the red box, CREATE ALERT.

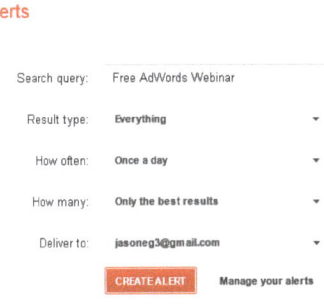

Even cooler, you can use the free Google Alerts to alert you to –

- **Informational items** based on keywords that matter to you and your company. For example, if you sell organic baby food, you can set up Google Alerts to alert you to new blog posts, web postings and other content relating to "organic baby food."

- Your **company name** – you can use Google Alerts to alert you to any mention of your company name, product name or other "branded search" keyword.

- **Speaking or writing opportunities** – for example, "call for papers" in your industry, or "guest blog" plus your target keywords to identify potential free publicity opportunities.

3

Google SEO

SEO, or Search Engine Optimization, is the art and science of getting to the top of Google and Bing, for free. If you sell industrial fans, for example, SEO is the art and science of getting your company and products at the top of relevant searches for industrial fans such as *industrial fans, industrial blowers, and industrial fans for agriculture. If you sell pizza in Palo Alto*, similarly, SEO is the art and science of getting your company to the top of Google and Google+ Local listings for *pizza, Italian food, Italian catering*, and other searches relating to pizza and Palo Alto.

SEO, in short, is the free stuff on Google to be contrasted with AdWords, which is the *paid* stuff.

Google actually has quite a few free resources on the topic of SEO for webmasters, marketers, and small business owners. They're there, but a bit hidden.

Why?

First and foremost, Google makes over 96% of its revenue from paid advertising (AdWords), so Google heavily promotes AdWords advertising as a solution to every marketing problem.

Google does not make money on SEO, so it does not promote the tactic with the same fervor for which it promotes advertising!

Second, Google's corporate culture is (ironically) terrible at details, i.e. at making stuff *easy to find*, so don't expect much cross-referencing (this is true even for AdWords, on which Google does make money). The left and right hand do not talk to each other at Google!

>> Google's Official SEO Guide

Google produces an informative, well-written guide to SEO called the "Search Engine Optimization Starter Guide." You can find it by Googling "Google SEO Guide," or just click to http://jm-seo.org/299-g15.

Get this guide, read this guide, and share this guide with your Web team! This guide is Google's **bible** as to how to do SEO properly! Some important points from the guide:

- Create unique and accurate (keyword-heavy) **TITLE tags** for all your web pages.

- **Avoid** numeric / **parameter-based URL's** in favor of keyword-heavy, static URL's.

- Use the **META DESCRIPTION tag** to accurately and uniquely describe page content.

The guide is also interesting for what it does not say. It does not address external link-building, the Penguin, Panda or other SEO penalties of recent years, nor social mentions – all of which are "off page" aspects of SEO that are incredibly important. Nonetheless, it's an official Google resource and a good guide for at least getting your "on page" SEO in order! So download and read Google's SEO Starter guide, today.

>> Google's Webmaster Tools

Google has an official program for webmasters called "Webmaster Tools." Here Google reaches out to webmasters and tries to share information on how to build SEO-friendly websites. You don't have to consider yourself a "webmaster" to join; all you have to have is your own website.

The program is free, and all you have to do is sign up and verify your site. You can find Webmaster tools at https://www.google.com/webmasters/. This site also has a cornucopia of information resources on how to build Google-friendly websites such as the Webmaster academy (http://jm-seo.org/299-g16) and Webmaster tools help (http://jm-seo.org/299-g17).

>> Google's Free SEO Tools

Google provides quite a few free tools to help with your SEO, especially in terms of keyword research, if you know where to look. The most important tool is the Google AdWords Keyword Planner (http://jm-seo.org/299-g18). My free video on how to use it is can be found at http://youtu.be/wwstmbQDsr8.

Another really good free Google keyword tool is called *Global Market Finder* at http://bit.ly/googplan. Just type your keywords into the box at the top right, click "find opportunity," then scroll down to the United States, click the "+" sign, then click the "+" sign again for English, and finally click the "show additional keyword suggestions from the keyword tool" link. It's a bit cumbersome, but this tool provides wonderful idea lists and volume data for relevant keywords.

Secondly, there is the Google trends service at http://www.google.com/trends which allows you to compare and contrast search term trends over time. Thirdly, with a little skill, you can use some Google tricks to get even more information on keywords used by your potential customers:

> **Google Suggest** – simply start typing in the Google search box at http://www.google.com/ and pay attention to the suggestions that show up in the pull-down; these are good indicators as to what consumers are typing into Google and therefore good SEO keyword targets.

> **Related Searches** – type in your basic keyword query into Google, hit enter, and then scroll to the very bottom of your screen. More often than not, you'll see a list of "related searches" there. Then click on any that intrigue you and repeat the process.

Here's a screen shot of "related searches" for "seo classes," again located at the very bottom of any Google search. Just click on any one of these terms to drill down to that related search term.

Google also has an important SEO tool called "Pagespeed insights" (http://jm-seo.org/299-g19) that will measure your website's speed and give helpful tips on how to speed it up. Website response speed is increasingly an important factor for achieving good SEO rank.

Finally, Google produces a free metrics platform called **Google Analytics** (http://www.google.com/analytics). **Google Analytics** is so important that I discuss it in detail in Chapter 8.

>> Google's Free SEO Tools

Since Google dominates search, it is important to pay attention to what official Googlers are saying about SEO. By far the most important individual is Matt Cutts, who can be followed on his blog (http://www.mattcutts.com/blog/) and Twitter (http://twitter.com/mattcutts). In terms of SEO, the other important official resources are the Webmaster tools blog (http://googlewebmastercentral.blogspot.com/) and YouTube channel (http://www.youtube.com/googlewebmasterhelp). As is always the case, don't expect the blog to tell you where the YouTube channel is, or for Matt Cutts to tell you where the official Webmaster resources are, and vice-versa. Remember: the left and right hand do not talk to each other at Google!

4

Google+ Local

Google+ Local, formerly called **Google Places**, is Google's alternative to the traditional *Yellow* Pages for local business search and a stiff competitor to site's like YellowPages.com or Yelp.com. A consumer who is looking for a local roofing company, for example, simply goes to Google and types in the keyword query "roofing company." Google knows their physical location from the computer's (or phone's) IP address and returns a list of relevant local companies in their area.

Today's busy consumers, whether on desktops, tablets, or mobile phones, often "Google" terms relating to local businesses and end up on Google+ Local via a Google search. In fact, many consumers use Google+ Local without realizing that it is distinct from Google itself.

For a user located in Dallas, Texas, here's a screen shot for the search query, "roofing company":

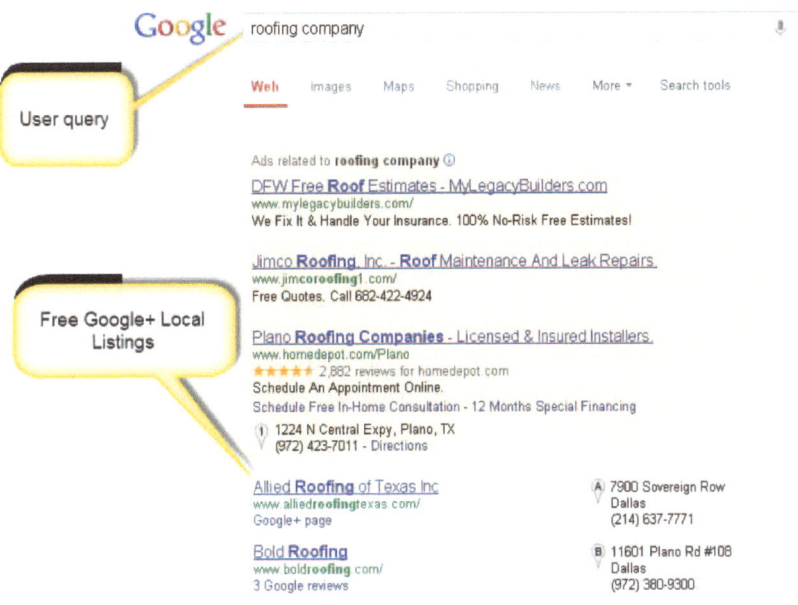

So what's the **free** opportunity here? Get your **free** listing on **Google+ Local** (http://www.google.com/business/placesforbusiness/) and be found by consumers in your area searching for your products or services by keywords. (If you don't have a website, Google will even give you one for free at http://www.gybo.com).

GOOGLE+ LOCAL IS A FREE BUSINESS LISTING ON GOOGLE

What's the catch? First of all, **free** company listings on **Google+ Local** occur in Google search *if, and only if,* Google determines that the user query has a local characteristic. In other words, the Google search engine is smart enough to figure out that certain types of queries are essentially like "Yellow Page" queries. When someone types in "pizza" or "divorce attorney" or "CPA Firm" Google interprets this search as a local search, and responds with company listings of those companies listed in the Google+ Local database.

For example, searches such as the following will usually generate Google+ Local results –

> *Pizza*
> *Divorce Attorney*
> *Roofing Companies*
> *Plumbers*
> *Home Health Care*
> *Homeless shelters*
> *CPAs*
> *Tax Accountants*
> *Sushi*
> *Italian Restaurants*
> *Christian Churches*

Second, your business gets to the top of these searches, if and only if, you have –

- **Claimed** your business listing; and/or

- **Optimized** your business listing for SEO; and/or

- **Cross-linked** your listing to/from your website; and/or

- Are receiving inbound **links** from other websites; and/or

- Have many **reviews** from customers; and/or

- Are "**better**" than competitors in the eyes of Google.

It's a **competitive** game, but with some knowledge and perseverance you can out-compete your competitors and get to the top of Google's **Google+ Local** listings for free!

Does Google+ Local matter for your business?

If you are local, the answer is YES.

It also depends on whether the types of queries your customers type into Google are recognized as **local searches**. The only way to tell is to go to Google and try entering search queries that your customers might enter (for example, "Dallas Roofing Company" or "Tulsa Attorneys" or just "roofing companies" or "attorney"). If you see local business listings (which are distinguished by a list of companies, with addresses and the little grey or red balloon marker), then **Google+ Local** is important to your business.

GOOGLE+ LOCAL = THE GOOGLE YELLOW PAGES

If your business is local, and if your potential customers use Google to find businesses like yours, **Google+ Local** should be a top priority in your Internet marketing strategy. What's more, **Google+ Local** is **free** for a basic listing, and with some tips and tricks, you have a shot at getting your company to appear at the top of the list, for **free**, for relevant Google queries!

>> Claim Your Free Google+ Local Listing

The good news is that your business probably already has a free listing on **Google+ Local**, even if you never set it up. That's because Google has built a massive database of businesses across the United States, Canada, and all over the world. The bad news is that businesses are listed whether they like it or not and consumers may be posting reviews, including bad reviews, about your business right now!

Google+ Local, therefore, is much more than the Yellow Pages online! It's a 24/7 consumer-generated **review machine** identifying favorite pizza parlors, divorce attorneys, roofing companies, home health care agencies, and more. If your business is local, **Google+ Local** is a make-or-break part of your free Internet marketing strategy.

Find or Claim Your Free Listing. Here's how you find (or claim) your free **Google+ Local** listing if you haven't already.

Method #1. Use Google maps.

1. Go to Google (http://www.google.com/). Type in "Google Maps" and hit enter. Alternatively, go directly to http://maps.google.com/.

2. Enter your business name and full address.

3. If your business exists, you will see it on the left side of the screen as well as marked by a red balloon marker.

4. Click on "reviews" or "Be the first to review."

5. After you click on "reviews," scroll about half way down on the resulting page and on the far right you will see an icon that says "Manage this page." Here's what that icon looks like:

6. Be sure you are "signed in" to your Google account (for example, the Gmail account of the business owner), and then follow the instructions to "claim" the listing. Usually Google will require postcard verification by mail for you to claim your listing.

Once you receive the official postcard, follow the instructions to enter your PIN and claim your listing.

At that point, you can optimize your listing by writing keyword-heavy but well-written text in your business description, upload photos of your business, and respond to customer reviews about your business.

Method #2. An alternative way to claim your **Google+ Local** listing is to go to http://www.google.com/business/placesforbusiness, sign in, and follow the instructions to claim a new business. Usually Google prefers that you use your phone number to claim a business in this fashion.

Here's a screenshot of what this looks like:

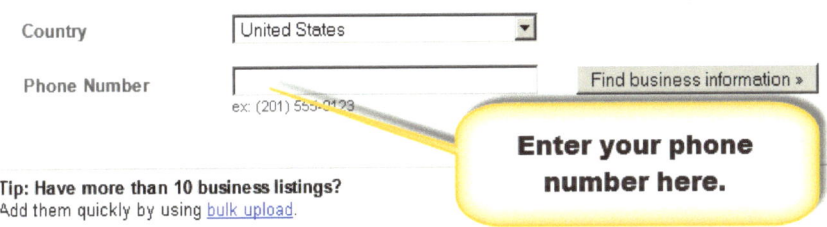

Tip: Before you create a business listing, think about which Google Account you are using. In the future, y business.

Enter your business's main phone number to see if Google Maps already has some information about your add new details, including photos and videos. About Google Places

| Country | United States ▼ |
| Phone Number | |

ex: (201) 555-0123

Find business information »

Enter your phone number here.

Tip: Have more than 10 business listings? Add them quickly by using bulk upload.

Once you have found your business, the process is same as Method #1.

Claiming your free business listing can be a hassle, but it only has to be done once, and then you have claimed it forever. Just be sure to write down the email address and password that corresponds to the Google account via which you claimed your Google+ Local listing. Don't lose the email address / password combination!

>> Optimize Your Free Google+ Local Listing

Now that you have claimed your **Google+ Local** listing, it's time to **optimize** it for local SEO. We teach an entire online class at the JM Internet Group (http://jm-seo.org/), but here are the basics:

1.   Sign into your Google account and your listing at http://www.google.com/business/placesforbusiness or if you have a Google+ page, log in to your Google+ page.

2.   Click "edit" on the far left of the listing within Places are far right of the screen in Google+. Here's a screenshot:

JM Internet Group

Fremont CA 94536
United States
Edit - Delete

Once you click "edit," you'll see your free business listing. Optimize your **business name** and **description** by writing keyword heavy text. If you are an Italian restaurant in Baltimore, for example, make sure that you describe all the specialties that you offer by keywords such as "Pizza," "Italian food" as well as perhaps "catering" and "party venue." Get the **target keywords** into your business description!

Note that you only have 200 characters, so use http://www.lettercount.com/ to pre-count the characters in your keyword-heavy Google+ Local listing.

Next, choose at least three existing Google categories in the **category** fields.

Here's a screenshot of what it looks like to enter your company information with the important items indicated by green arrows:

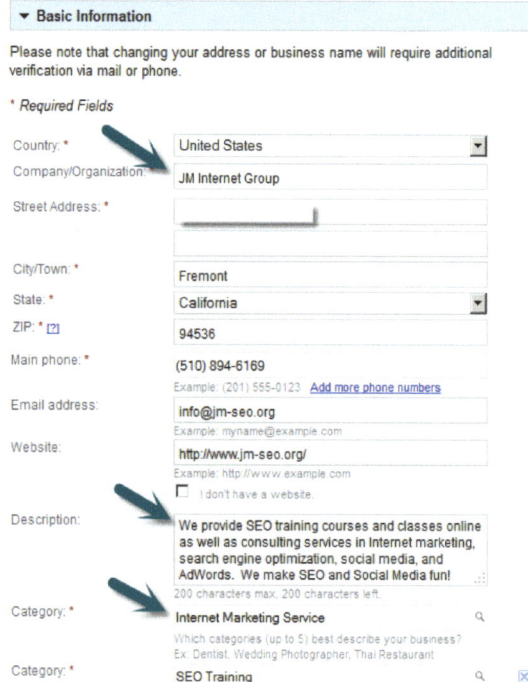

Recently, Google has consolidated Google+ with Google+ local, and so in some cases your Google+ local listing will be a subordinate component of your Google+ page for your business. In that case, just make sure to enter a physical address when you set up your Google+ page for your business. The reviews will occur under the "about" tab on your Google+ page.

If you do not have a consolidated Google+ / Google+ Local page for your business, you can end up with two pages (one for Google+ and one for Google+ Local). That's OK as well.

There are other tricks and tips to perfect local SEO optimization for **Google+ Local**, but those are the basics.

Get Customer Reviews. Once you have claimed and optimized your free **Google+ Local** listing the challenge becomes getting happy customers to review you. How do you get reviews?

In a nutshell: **ask**.

Make it a part of your business process that when you encounter a happy customer, you (or your employees) simply ask them to "do you a favor" and go to Google+ Local and write an honest review.

And make it easy for them to review you. One helpful free technique is to shorten your terribly long Google+ Local URL to make it user friendly. To do this, copy your long URL into a a free URL shortener like http://bit. ly or http://goo.gl. Then you can print or email the short URL to clients when you ask them for reviews.

For example, here are the two URLs for the JM Internet Group –

Long URL. https://plus.google.com/100991455660382254177/about

Shortened URL. http://bit.ly/jmgplus

A simple email to a happy customer might say:

```
Greetings!

Thank you for the opportunity to serve you on
your {fill-in-the-blank} needs.

If you have a moment, please do us a huge favor
and review us on Google+ Local, Google's local
listing site.

To do so:

    1. Go to http://bit.ly/jmgplus (Replace with
    your own shortened URL).
    2. Click on "Write a review".
    3. You may be prompted to "sign in" to your
    Google account, or to create one.
    4. Write your honest review.

Thank you in advance for helping our business.

Best regards,
The Management
```

(If you like this book, feel free to go to our own Google+ Local page above and write a review. But in your own situation, be sure to replace our bit.ly shortened URL with a direct link to your own Google+ Local listing).

The shortened URL is easy to print on flyers or send out in emails. So use one of these free tools to shorten your URL, and then print some card or email reminders for those happy customers to log on and write positive reviews about your business.

Businesses that a) **claim** their free listings, b) **optimize** those listings by including target keyword searches, and c) have **many** positive **reviews** tend to be the ones that rank high on relevant local searches on Google.

>> Free Google+ Local Resources

Once you have the basics of Google+ Local under control, you will want to educate yourself on the ins and outs of successful local SEO marketing. Here are some of the better free Google+ Local resources to help you master Google+ Local. First and foremost, know and use the primary URL of Google+ Local (http://www.google.com/business/placesforbusiness/) to actively manage your company listing. Second, go to the Google+ Local user's guide at http://jm-seo.org/299-g1. The user's guide has many question and answer posts to commonly asked questions about Google+ Local. Third, use the Google+ Local online help at http://jm-seo.org/299-g2. Note that the user's guide and the help guide is not the same thing! Finally, keep informed about goings-on at Google+ Local at their official home page at http://www.google.com/+/business/.

5

Google+

Google+ (pronounced "Google Plus") is Google's competitive challenge to Facebook, a social network platform wherein individuals can have "profiles" and businesses can have "pages." (**Google+ Local** is part of Google+, but is really more like Yelp, Citysearch, or Angie's list, and was discussed in Chapter 4.)

You might think that Google+ is not very important, because few people outside of the tech community really use Google+. But remember that Google+ has a very powerful sponsor – **Google**, a sponsor that is doing everything in its power to grow this new social network.

I like to think of Google as "daddy" and Google+ as its new, beloved "baby." You can bet that Google is using its available resources to help out Google+, among them priority on the Google search engine to organizations that embrace Google+. Don't forget that Google also owns YouTube, and can be expected to use YouTube to help Google+ as well. The recent fact that one must now use Google+ to comment on YouTube is an example of the "Google family" helping out its newest member.

Let's investigate.

>> Google+ for Individuals

Ironically, while Google+ has pages for businesses, the most important **free** opportunity for *businesses* on Google+ actually occurs at the *individual* level. If you (or a "guru" of your business) set up an active Google+ personal profile, and cross-link that account correctly to your website, you can get your picture to show up on Google searches. For example, here's a search for "Chicago SEO Class" showing my picture in the free, organic results on a Google search:

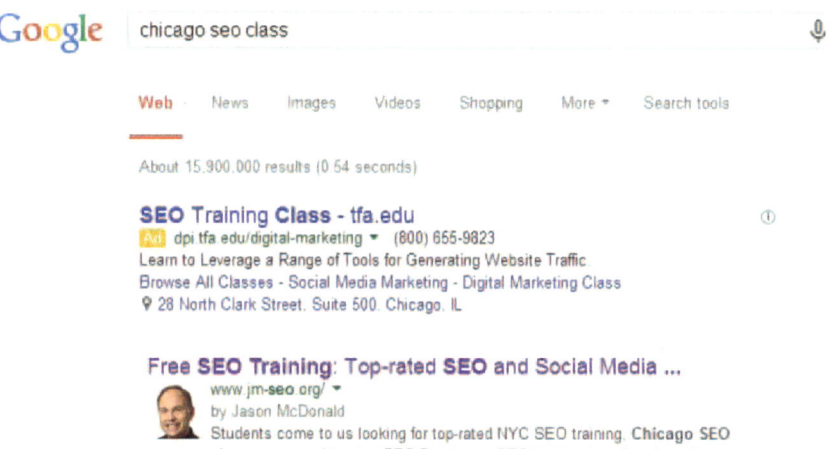

What's great about Google+ personal is that, if you have uploaded a personal photo, correctly attached it to your website, and built enough positive "buzz" on Google+, Google will frequently show your picture next to search results. Besides looking cool and making you seem like an authority in your industry, this tends to increase your click through rate. Subsequently, the more people that follow you on Google+, the more your picture shows, the more you get clicks... thereby creating a **virtuous circle** on Google!

Here are the basic set-up steps for a Google+ personal profile:

1.   Log into your Google or Gmail account at http://www.google.com/ (top right of screen).

2.   Click the 9 dots at the top right of the screen (which looks like a telephone key pad), and then scroll down to Google+.

3.   Follow the steps to set up a basic personal Google+ profile.

Be sure to fill out a keyword-heavy profile, and encourage as many friends, family, and customers to circle you on Google+ (by having them login to their own Google+ account, find your account, and then "add to circles").

After you have set up your personal Google+, you then need to enable "authorship." This is pretty complicated, so follow the detailed instructions on this tutorial post at http://www.jm-seo.org/26. You can also read Google's own instructions at http://jm-seo.org/299-g10. Once you have cross-linked your personal Google+ account to your website, use

Google's free "structured data testing tool" (http://jm-seo.org/299-g20) to verify you did it correctly.

Next, get people to "circle" you on Google+, post frequently on relevant topics, and cross-pollinate Google+ and your blog. These factors combine to determine when Google will show your picture next to relevant search results. Getting your picture to show, for free, on Google is a great way to stand out on Google search and increase the click through rate from Google to your website!

>> Google+ for Business

Businesses can get on Google+ as well, but they cannot get their pictures to show on search results. With few engaged users compared with Facebook, Google+ is currently a limited marketing opportunity at the purely business level.

Google+ for business may still be worth setting up, however, because, since Google owns Google+, there is no doubt that it will tilt search results to favor businesses that participate in the network. (*Sorry to be such a cynic!*).

Setting up a Google+ Page for your business is free, and easy. Google+ for business is at http://www.google.com/+/business/. It can be confusing, so keep in mind that three very different products are available under the Google+ umbrella:

- **Google+ for Business.** Think of this as Google's alternative to Facebook **pages** for business at http://www.google.com/+/business/.

- **Google+ for Individuals.** Think of this as Google's alternative to Facebook profiles for individuals, with the big opportunity being getting your picture to show on Google searches at http://plus.google.com/.

- **Google+ Local.** Think of this as Google's Internet Yellow Pages, competitive to **Yelp** at http://www.google.com/places.

Finally, remember that Google+ and Google+ local can be separate or combined; so your business may have one interface to manage both, or two separate interfaces, one for each one. Simplicity is not a guiding light at Google!

Returning to Google+ for business, a Google+ page for your business can impact your brand identity. It will often show at the top right of searches for your company name. Here's a screenshot of the search for "National Geographic, for example:"

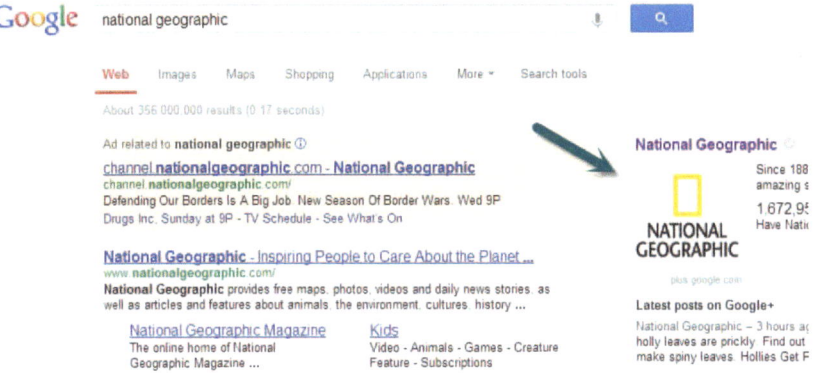

A similar pattern will often occur with businesses that have robust Google+ Local pages. Search Google for the business name, and on the right you'll often see the Google+ Local listing.

Finally, you can and should enhance your website with the following free plug-in's available at https://developers.google.com/+/plugins/. Both are thought to help your Google search rankings:

> **Google+1 Button** – allow users to "+1" your website, thereby casting a virtual vote that your website is cool, and possibly having a small positive effect on your SEO performance.

> **Google+ Badge** – allow users who are on Google+ to "circle" your company's own Google+ website (akin to "liking" a page on Facebook).

If your business has strong video components, you might check out Google+ Hangouts (http://www.google.com/+/learnmore/hangouts/), which is arguably the most innovative feature on Google+.

You can browse Google+ help at http://jm-seo.org/299-g21 and learn more, generally, about how Google+ works at http://www.google.com/+/learnmore/.

YouTube

YouTube, owned by Google, is both a learning resource about other free Google opportunities, and a free opportunity in its own right. Many small business owners think of YouTube as the province of Lady Gaga, Justin Bieber, and stupid pet jokes, while missing out on YouTube as an incredibly valuable free business resource.

>> YouTube as a Free Learning Resource

Whether it is Google Analytics, AdWords, or Webmaster tools, you can almost always find both official and non-official videos that explain step-by-step tools and opportunities across the GooglePlex. For a list of all official Google YouTube channels go to http://jm-seo.org/299-g26. Once there, select "For all regions" to see the most important Google channels on YouTube:

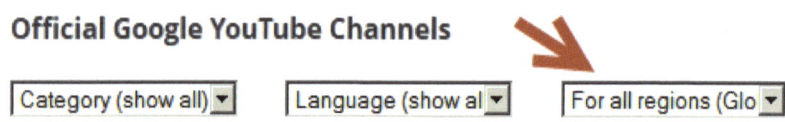

Beyond the official list of official Google YouTube channels, you can simply search YouTube for videos, simply go to YouTube (http://www.youtube.com/) and enter search terms such as "Google Analytics" or "What is a Landing Page in Google Analytics," or "How do I claim a free business listing on Google?" into the search box. Next, click on "filter," to filter the results. Two good filters are "last month" (for recent videos) and "view count" for most popular. Here is a screenshot of the filter tab opened:

Finally, you can go to Google itself and type in a search query such as "What is Bounce Rate" and hit enter. Then select "Videos" in the thin band at the top, or click "enter" as for example: Finally, you can use the "site:" command in Google and type *site:youtube.com* plus your search query as follows:

 site:youtube.com bounce rate

Remember that there is no space between site: and *youtube*, so its *site:youtube.com* not *site: youtube.com*. Any of these advanced search techniques is a good way to use YouTube to identify "how to" videos on topics that can help your small business marketing efforts.

>> YouTube as a Trend Watcher

Trends on the Internet often hit YouTube first, and if your business depends on consumer trends, YouTube is one of the best free platforms to monitor consumer trends. The first way to watch trends is to enter your search keywords at http://www.youtube.com/ and then click the "filter" button. Here is an example of a YouTube search for "carbon offsets" after clicking on the "filters" button and then clicking on "view count:"

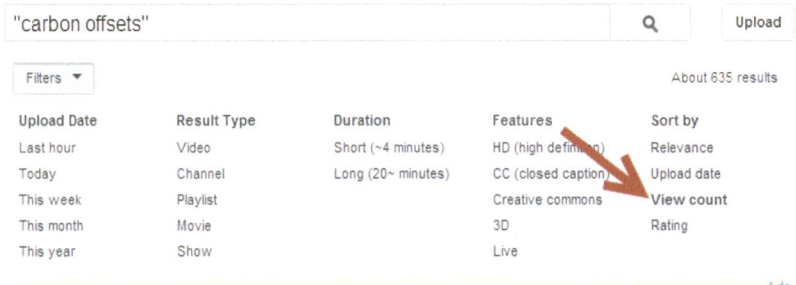

You can also filter for "this month," for example, and thereby find the most popular videos on a topic for the most recent month.

Other YouTube trend resources are somewhat hidden. For example, you can watch trending and most popular videos via YouTube Charts (http://jm-seo.org/299-g27). Next, scroll down and you'll see categories such as sports, the daily 'Aww,' and other pop-culture themes. YouTube also has a blog on YouTube trends at http://youtube-trends.blogspot.com/, admittedly focusing largely on pop culture as well as a trends dashboard where you can filter by demographic age groups and sex (http://www.youtube.com/trendsdashboard). Finally, YouTube has its own version of the keyword tool (https://www.youtube.com/keyword_tool) which shows you keyword searches on YouTube by popularity.

>> Creating Your Own YouTube Channel for Free

YouTube, of course, is a **free** marketing opportunity in its own right. Any business can set up its own YouTube channel, for free, and then post videos to that channel. Most small businesses will simply want to sign up for an individual YouTube account "as a business" and then populate their channel with background images, explanatory text, links to their website, and of course videos. You can learn more about this process at http://jm-seo.org/299-g28 and you can also build out a "brand" channel (which has an advertising component) at http://jm-seo.org/299-g29.

Once you've begun the process of creating your own channel, don't miss YouTube creator's corner (http://www.youtube.com/t/creators_corner), a free and helpful resource on video production. The YouTube help files are a bit hidden at http://support.google.com/youtube/ but like all Google help, once you know where it's located, you can simply type in your question and find a ton of useful articles on any problem you are having with YouTube. YouTube also has a "product forum" (http://jm-seo.org/299-g30) where users can ask other users and official YouTubers for help on various issues.

YouTube has very good, free, analytics tool about your video engagement, but it is quite buried as well. Here's how to find YouTube analytics:

Sign into your YouTube account. Next, click on your avatar at the top right of the screen, and then video manager:

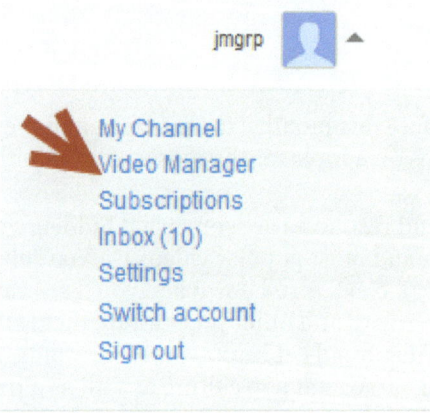

After you have opened up video manager, click on the little graph icon to the right of any video to see engagement statistics for that video:

Then on the left column, you can click on any number of metrics such as views, playback locations, and traffic sources. YouTube's metrics are quite good but they have unfortunately buried them many clicks below, and quite a few YouTubers don't know how to find them!

>> YouTube Learning Resources

YouTube, of course, has its own YouTube channel (http://www.youtube.com/user/youtube), its own blog (http://youtube-global.blogspot.com/), and YouTube creator's blog (http://youtubecreator.blogspot.com/). As for other social media, you can of course "like" YouTube on Facebook (https://www.facebook.com/youtube) and "follow" YouTube on Twitter (https://twitter.com/youtube), and "circle" YouTube on Google+ (https://plus.google.com/+youtube/posts). Unfortunately, YouTube tends to mix its consumer oriented content and its content oriented at "content creators," so you have to read through a lot of the former to get to the latter.

>> YouTube Advertising

Google makes its money off of advertising, and so does YouTube. So if video advertising might be good for your business, start off with their free resources to learn about how to advertise on YouTube. There is a guide to advertising on YouTube called "YouTube for Business" (http://www.youtube.com/yt/advertise/) as well as a YouTube channel on advertising and marketing (https://www.youtube.com/user/advertise).

Confusingly, YouTube advertising actually "lives" inside of AdWords, so if you actually do advertise on YouTube you will be managing that inside of AdWords (http://adwords.google.com/).

7

AdWords

AdWords is Google's *pay-per-click* advertising program, wherein advertisers submit bids as to how much they are willing to pay for a "click" from Google to their website based on keywords. In addition to Google or the "Search Network," AdWords can also place your ads across blogs, YouTube, Gmail, and other sites via what is called the "Display Network."

Like so much at Google, AdWords is both powerful and complicated. What's particularly stressful about AdWords is that a small business owner can easily churn through a lot of money, fast, without getting good results if they don't know what they are doing.

Fortunately, Google produces many good learning resources and tools for AdWords, if you know where to look.

>> AdWords Learning Resources

Before you get started with AdWords, or perhaps even if you have already started, take advantage of the plethora of free AdWords learning resources. They are informative, if a bit sales oriented, so I recommend you also sign up for my free online AdWords class at http://www.jm-seo. org/free. Here are the free official Google AdWords learning resources:

> **Learn with Google** – this is a good, introductory sales pitch in video format from Google about online marketing and advertising, especially AdWords, located at http://www.google.com/ads/learn/. Another similar site is at http://www.google.com/ads/experienced/. Be sure to not miss the items at the very bottom such as "search ads" or "video ads."

> **Google Ads: Ad Innovations** – this is a splashy site that shares the newer innovations from Google for its

advertising platforms such as search, display, and video at http://www.google.com/ads/innovations/.

Creative Sandbox by Google – prepare to be dazzled, as this is a very flashy overview of all the advertising opportunities across the Googleplex at http://www.creativesandbox.com/guidebook.

Learn with Google (Free) Webinars – these are more advanced in-depth presentations, taught live in Webinar format, and are not just AdWords but all sorts of Google-related issues such as Google Analytics at http://jm-seo.org/299-g22.

AdWords Seminars for Success are "real world" paid seminars that travel the World, introducing businesses to AdWords in courses 101, 201, 301, and 301. More at http://jm-seo.org/299-g23.

Please note that I produce both a free book on AdWords and a free online tutorial, available at http://www.jm-seo.org/free. These are independent tutorials on how to use AdWords without wasting a lot of money.

Finally, Google produces some good content about day-to-day trends and news for AdWords advertisers on the official AdWords blog (http://adwords.blogspot.com/) and the Google Business channel on YouTube (http://www.youtube.com/user/GoogleBusiness). You can also "friend" Google AdWords on Facebook at https://www.facebook.com/adwords.

>> AdWords Engage (Certification)

If you are an ad agency or web designer, you might consider becoming AdWords certified (http://jm-seo.org/299-g24). This program allows you to become an officially certified AdWords partner at either the individual or company level, and provides co-op marketing support from Google. It is, therefore, both a learning and a sales program, so expect the official Google line on AdWords rather than a more critical, third-party approach to AdWords.

Parallel to the official certification program is "Engage for Agencies." This is a more relaxed sales-oriented program to help ad agencies and web designers sell more companies on using Google AdWords. It has both marketing and educational resources such as free webinars. You can find it at http://www.google.com/ads/engage/.

>> AdWords Help

Once you have started an ad campaign on AdWords, you might want to know where to find "help." First and foremost, don't forget that "help" is located in the upper right hand corner of the AdWords software, hidden beneath the "gear" icon:

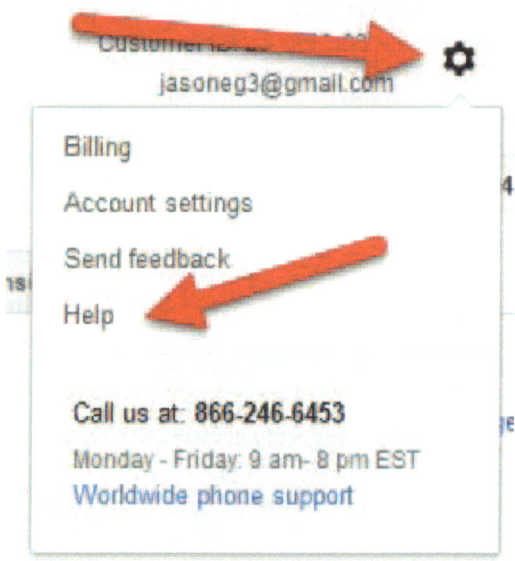

You can also search AdWords help directly at http://support.google.com/adwords/. Don't miss the "AdWords community" at https://www.en.adwords-community.com/ where you can post your burning questions about AdWords and get help from official Googlers or other AdWords gurus.

>> AdWords

Google produces some nifty tools to help you with AdWords, especially with respect to keywords. The most important is the *Google AdWords Keyword Planner*, which can be found inside of AdWords by clicking on "Tools" and then "Keyword Planner." This tool can give you keyword ideas, volume and value as measured by bids by competitors to get clicks from Google to your website. As such it offers invaluable insight into user behavior.

It is, unfortunately, difficult to use, so I recommend you watch my video tutorial on how to use the keyword planner at http://youtu.be/wwstmbQDsr8.

Returning to the "tools" tab in AdWords, notice a few other important tools. Google Analytics is an incredible metrics tool (dealt with in Chapter 8). Another useful tool here is the *Display Planner*. This tool allows you to preview possible ad placements on the Google Display Network, and is an easy way to find blogs, portals, and other websites that talk about your industry that might offer free publicity opportunities. Other tools such as *Ad Preview and Diagnosis* are very focused and useful if you have a specific issue inside of AdWords. The important thing to remember is that all the AdWords tools are on the "Tools" tab.

If you are an agency, have a complex AdWords account, or need to share information with your team, don't miss the free AdWords Editor (http://jm-seo.org/299-g25), which is an offline version of the AdWords interface.

8

Google Analytics

Google Analytics is Google's free web metrics platform. Beyond being by Google, for Google, and about Google, it's not only free but also powerful. It's become the choice for web metrics for businesses, small and large. Google Analytics can tell you how people get to your website (for example, via Google search, via social media sites like Facebook or Twitter, via press releases, via advertising or via other sources of traffic). And Google Analytics can tell you what people do once they land, from the top landing pages to the page browsing patterns to whether they actually buy anything or register as a sales lead. Smart marketers want accurate data on web visitor behavior, and Google Analytics gives you this for free.

Signing up for Google Analytics is your first step, and your second step is to discover the cornucopia of free learning information on Google Analytics. Let's investigate.

>> Anaytics Basics

Getting started with Google Analytics is easy. First, sign in to your Google or Gmail account, and go to http://www.google.com/analytics. Follow the instructions there to sign up for Analytics and get the all-important Javascript tracking code that you must place on each and every page of your website. (For detailed instructions on how to install the tracking code, go to http://bit.ly/ga-tracking). Once you have placed the tracking code on every page of your website, Google Analytics will track how users come to your website and what they do once they arrive – all for free!

>> Analytics Learning Resources

Although Analytics can be easy to set up, it isn't necessarily easy to use. The user interface is confusing, and riddled with esoteric terms and hidden clickable links that can confuse a novice user. Fortunately, Google provides a wealth of free learning resources. Start first with "help" which is hidden beneath the "gear" icon located at the top right of the screen inside of Google Analytics:

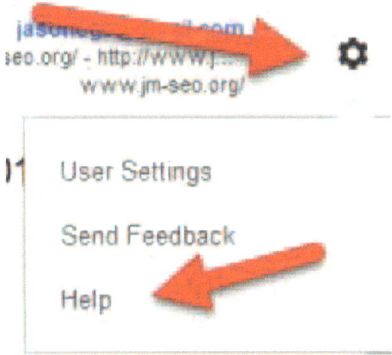

If you have a question about anything regarding Google Analytics, just first click on the "help" button, and then type your question. Presto! You'll find answers from Google help.

You can also browse or search Google Analytics help, directly, at http:// support.google.com/analytics/ and don't forget to just go to Google and search for any burning question you have about Google Analytics. If, for example, you don't understand what a landing page is inside of Google Analytics, just type "Landing Page" into the Google Analytics help search. Don't know the difference between a "sessions" and a "user?" Type "Visitor" into the help search. It's so simple, yet so many people forget to use the available online help files.

For those who learn by video, Google produces a fabulous micro site called *Google Analytics Academy* which has free video trainings on topics such as filters, e-commerce, sub-domains vs. domains, and even how to install the tracking code. To find it from within Google Analytics, first click on the "hat" icon on the far right, then click on "Analytics Academy" on the left, and finally to the link to http://analyticsacademy. withgoogle.com/. Alternatively, just go to http://jm-seo.org/299-g31. Once there you can not only watch informative training videos, you can sign up for a test to become officially certified in Google Analytics for a modest fee. That's great if you are a web designer or consultant offering services in web metrics.

The official Google Analytics product forum (http://jm-seo.org/299-g32) is another good learning resource. Post a question and get a response from other Google Analytics users or even an official Googler. And if you have a good budget, Google runs official Google Analytics learning seminars across the country at http://bit.ly/gaseminar with a cost of about $450 for Analytics 101, 201, and 301 (each).

>> Analytics Apps and Developer Resources

Analytics offers an ecosystem of free and paid apps similar to Google Play for the masses. You can check out the App Gallery at http://www.google.com/analytics/apps or the marketplace at http://jm-seo.org/299-g33. The latter is more focused on companies and services.

If you have your own web developer, you can point him/her to the Google Developers site for Analytics at https://developers.google.com/analytics/ but recommend that he/she check the App Gallery first to see if someone else has already invented an "app for that."

Official Googlers who are nuts for Google Analytics run an impressive system of blogs and social media accounts, but as is generally true at Google, the left and the right hand do not communicate. Start, of course, at the Google Analytics official blog (http://analytics.blogspot.com/) but you can also follow Google Analytics' official team members on social media as follows:

> **Twitter** at https://twitter.com/googleanalytics

> **Facebook** at http://www.facebook.com/GoogleAnalytics

> **Google+** at https://plus.google.com/+GoogleAnalytics/

> **YouTube** at http://www.youtube.com/googleanalytics

9

Googling Googlers

A **Googler** is technically a person who works at Google, but in terms of free Google resources for small business, we focus in this chapter on "Googling Googlers," meaning information resources to help you keep up-to-date, for **free**, about all the Google opportunities and changes that might have an impact on your business.

You would think that there would be a master resource of all the Google information channels, but there isn't. The left and the right hand do not talk to each other at Google! So in this chapter we will overview the various blogs, Twitter feeds, and other resources by Google, about Google.

If any of the Google properties matter to your business, you'll want to keep informed of opportunities and policy changes coming from the Googleplex.

Here's how.

>> Google Blogs

Almost every Google media property – AdWords, Google Webmaster tools, Google+ – has an official **blog**. The trick is to know to look for it, find it, and then bookmark or even subscribe to it via RSS so that you are kept informed of any and all opportunities or policy changes.

Before you start, let me alert you to a non-Google RSS (blog) reader called **Feedly** (http://www.feedly.com/). For unknown reasons, Google killed its own RSS reader, *Google Reader*, but fortunately Feedly came along and – for free – can be used to subscribe to various Google blogs. Feedly makes it easy to keep up with your favorite blogs, including of course official Google blogs. So first, sign up for Feedly, and give it permission to access your Gmail or Google Account at installation. Then, as you find blogs of interest add them to Feedly by clicking on "Add Content" at the top left of the screen.

With Feedly installed, we can turn to the official blogs by Google, about Google.

Google has a master list of all official Google blogs at http://jm-seo. org/299-g4. Some of the most important are:

- **Google AdWords Blog** (http://adwords.blogspot.com/)

- **Google Analytics Blog** (http://analytics.blogspot.com/)

- **Google Webmaster Central Blog** (http://googlewebmastercen-tral.blogspot.com/)

To subscribe to a blog, simply click on the "Add Content" button at the top left of Feedly and follow the instructions there, or look for the RSS feed (usually an orange icon) on the blog, and follow the relevant instructions. With a little back-and-forth, you'll be able to add the most relevant blogs to your Feedly account. I recommend you group them into categories inside Feedly such as Advertising, SEO, or Social Media.

>> Google Twitter, Google+, and Facebook Feeds

Just as with blogs, Google provides a cornucopia of information on social media (Twitter, Google+, Facebook) about SEO, AdWords, Google Analytics, Webmaster Tools, etc. The question is how to find all those Google Twitter feeds. Don't expect the *Webmaster Tools Twitter* feed to tell you where the *AdWords Twitter feed* is – of course!

But there is a nice directory of all official Google Twitter feeds at http:// jm-seo.org/299-g5. And many of the Twitter feeds are pretty easy to guess such as AdWords (https://twitter.com/adwords), Analytics (https://twitter.com/googleanalytics), Google Webmaster Tools (https:// twitter.com/googlewmc) or Official Google (https://twitter.com/google).

A Twitter account is free of course so your steps are:

1. Sign up for a free Twitter account at http://twitter.com/.

2. "Follow" your favorite Google accounts.

3. Periodically log in to Twitter and see what's being shared by your favorite Googlers.

As for **Google+**, it isn't the strongest social network but of course it's by Google for Google, so naturally it's a good place to look to stay informed about what's going on at Google for small business. Google has a directory of official Google+ feeds at http://jm-seo.org/299-g6. Ironically, not all of the most important Google properties are listed on that feed, so sometimes you have to search for them. Here are some of the most important:

- **AdWords** (https://plus.google.com/+GoogleAds/posts)

- **Google Analytics** (https://plus.google.com/+GoogleAnalytics/posts)

- **Google Webmaster Tools** (https://plus.google.com/+GoogleWebmasters/posts)

- **Official Google** (https://plus.google.com/+google/posts)

Here's a trick you can use on Google search to find relevant content on Google+.

- Go to http://www.google.com/.

- Type in to the Google search box this exact phrase:

  site:plus.google.com

- Then enter a search query such as "Google AdWords Official" as in

  site:plus.google.com Google AdWords Official

By doing this, you are using Google to search Google+ and can often find the official channels you are looking for in this fashion. You can also log in directly to Google+ at http://plus.google.com/ and use the search box there.

Is Google on **Facebook**? Of course Google is on Facebook, and you can find a complete list of official Google Facebook pages at http://jm-seo.org/299-g7. Among the most important are Google AdWords (http://www.facebook.com/adwords), Google Analytics (http://www.facebook.com/GoogleAnalytics), and YouTube (http://www.facebook.com/youtube).

>> Google on YouTube

In terms of keeping up with Google opportunities, nothing really matches YouTube. In many cases, what a small business owner or marketer is looking for is a "how to" video on Google AdWords, Google+ for business, or how to use Google Analytics. YouTube is the place to look for informative "how to" videos. You can find a directory of Google YouTube channels at http://jm-seo.org/299-g8.

Among the most important are the official Google YouTube channel (http://www.youtube.com/Google) as well as Google Analytics (http://www.youtube.com/googleanalytics) and Google Webmaster Tools (http://www.youtube.com/GoogleWebmasterHelp). The most important by far is the Google Business channel (http://www.youtube.com/Google-Business) which posts many informative videos about Google's business products. Curiously, AdWords does not seem to have its own YouTube channel but posts instead to Google Business!

>> Important Googlers

Some individual Googlers are so important that you should pay attention to their activity on Social Media. First and foremost is Matt Cutts, head of the Web spam team at Google. You can follow Cutts' blog at http://www.mattcutts.com/blog/ and on Twitter at https://twitter.com/mattcutts. Another important Googler is Maile Ohye at http://maileohye.com/ or on Twitter at https://twitter.com/maileohye. Neither is very active on Google+ (though you can follow Cutts at http://plus.google.com/+MattCutts/posts), at least in a professional sense, but you can find them by searching for their names by typing *site:plus.google.com* into Google.

>> More Google Resources – The Bonus Appendix

This guide has presented the wealth of free information on Google by Google, topic by topic, but we are always discovering new Google resources just as Google is always creating new ones. To get a complete, organized list of resources, you can obtain the **Bonus Appendix** by writing a review of this guide, blogging it, or sharing it with a Tweet.

Simply go to http://jm-seo.org/299 and follow the instructions there, or give us a call at 510-713-2150.

Happy Googling!

~ Jason McDonald, Ph.D.

About The Author

About the Author. Jason McDonald, Ph.D., teaches SEO and Social Media online for the JM Internet Group. He has coached thousands of businesspeople, marketers, and web designers in his free online classes as well as paid seminars and corporate trainings. Just Google 'Jason McDonald' to find his Website or send him a message – he's No. 1 on Google!